THE JACKSONIAN

THE JACKSONIAN

⊱ A PLAY ⊰

BETH HENLEY

NORTHWESTERN UNIVERSITY PRESS

EVANSTON, ILLINOIS

Northwestern University Press
www.nupress.northwestern.edu

ISBN 978-0-8101-3065-4 (paper)
ISBN 978-0-8101-3066-1 (e-book)

Library of Congress Cataloging-in-Publication data are available from the Library of Congress.

♾ The paper used in this publication meets the minimum requirements of the American National Standard for Information Sciences—Permanence of Paper for Printed Library Materials, ANSI Z39.48-1992.

To my nephew Craig and to Mama

CONTENTS

ACKNOWLEDGMENTS

I want to especially thank the actors who have collaborated with me since the play was first read in my living room: Ed Harris, Amy Madigan, Bill Pullman, and Glenne Headly. (Glenne Headly, Glenne Headly, Glenne Headly!)

Thank you, Holly Hunter, Dominique Hinman, and Joe Clark, for the readings at my home that you participated in so enthusiastically.

I'm grateful to Carol Kane and Bill Pullman for coming over to my house with brazen encouragement that led to the development of the play at New York Stage and Film.

Thank you, Johanna Pfaelzer, for always saying yes.

My deep appreciation to Gil Cates and Randy Arney for taking a brave chance and giving the play its first production.

Immeasurable thanks to Frank Levering for getting the play to Ian.

Deep thanks to Scott Elliot, Geoff Rich, Ian Morgan, and the New Group for the uncompromising love your company gave to the New York production.

Richard Bausch and Jon Parrish Peede (publisher, *Virginia Quarterly Review*), I am so grateful for your early and staunch belief in this play.

My heartfelt thanks to LMU/LA for its generous and continuing support and to my inspiring colleagues in the Theatre Arts and Dance Departments.

Ongoing thanks to Belita Moreno, Mona Simpson, Colleen Dodson-Baker, Camilla Carr, Bob Dolman, Ron Marasco, and Brian Shuff for standing close by through the waxing and waning of my work on this play and others.

Thank you, Peter Hagan, for helping me lift this play and many more off the ground and up onto the stage.

Robert Falls, through your patience, theatrical acumen, and unobtrusive genius, you helped me find the play I was longing to write.

And finally, deep love and thanks to Cherry Dude (who dearly knows me) and Patrick Henley, my beloved son and long-time supporter.

PRODUCTION HISTORY

New York Stage and Film Company, with Johanna Pfaelzer as artistic director, presented a reading of *The Jacksonian* in 2009.

The Jacksonian was originally produced in Los Angeles by Geffen Playhouse (Gilbert Cates, producing director; Randall Arney, artistic director; Ken Novice; managing director) in February 2012. It was directed by Robert Falls; scenic design was by Walt Spangler; costume design was by Ana Kuzmanic; lighting design was by Daniel Ionazzi; the composer and sound designer was Richard Woodbury; the fight coordinator was Ned Mochel; and the production stage manager was Young Ji.

The cast was as follows:

Rosy Perch	Bess Rous
Bill Perch	Ed Harris
Eva White	Glenne Headly
Fred Weber	Bill Pullman
Susan Perch	Amy Madigan

The Jacksonian was originally produced in New York City by the New Group (Scott Elliot, artistic director; Geoff Rich, executive director; Ian Morgan, associate artistic director) in October 2013. It was directed by Robert Falls; scenic design was by Walt Spangler; costume design was by Ana Kuzmanic; lighting design was by Daniel Ionazzi; the composer and sound designer was Richard Woodbury; the fight coordinator was Ned Mochel; and the production stage manager was Valerie A. Wright.

The cast was as follows:

Rosy Perch	Juliet Brett

Bill Perch . . . . Ed Harris
Eva White. . . . . Glenne Headly
Fred Weber . . . . Bill Pullman
Susan Perch . . . . Amy Madigan

THE JACKSONIAN

CHARACTERS

Rosy Perch, daughter of Bill and Susan Perch
Bill Perch, a dentist and motel resident
Eva White, a waitress and motel maid
Fred Weber, the motel bartender
Susan Perch, Bill Perch's wife and the mother of Rosy

SETTING

The action of the play takes place at the Jacksonian Motel, an establishment on the outskirts of Jackson, Mississippi.

The motel exists as a haunting memory, a sort of purgatory that was Jackson, Mississippi, circa 1964.

There are three playing spaces: the bar/restaurant; a motel room; and the outside ice machine.

The Rosy monologues are direct address. Evoked by murder, Rosy's will and terror quake the landscape of the time, space, and memory.

In these monologues, Rosy may break theatrical conventions that are established for the rest of the play.

TIME

March 1964–December 1964

The scenes are not played linearly.

SCENE 1: THERE'S BEEN AN ACCIDENT

[*The Jacksonian Motel. Time: the night of the murder—December 17, 1964. Lights up on* ROSY PERCH, *age sixteen. She wears pajamas and is wrapped in a blanket.*]

ROSY: There's been an accident—there's going to be—I need to stop an accident at the motel. The Jacksonian Motel.

[ROSY *watches as* BILL PERCH *enters holding an ice bucket and goes to the ice machine. He has blood on his hands and shirt.* PERCH *violently digs the ice bucket into the ice. There is the sound of ice crashing. He holds the ice in the bucket and stares out for no more than a moment.* PERCH *exits.*]

We need to leave.

We need to leave in time.

The time is—What time is—

[*The following lines overlap as* FRED WEBER *enters from behind the bar and* EVA WHITE *enters and stands by the bar with menace.*]

It's not Christmas. It's near around before—before Christmas.

There is a Christmas tree at the motel. But it is not the real tree.

The real tree is at home.

And it is before—

Before a time that makes the time of murder.

[*A bar/restaurant at the Jacksonian Motel. Time: the night of the murder—December 17, 1964. There is a manger scene and a string of Christmas lights. EVA is staring coldly across space. FRED is smoking a cigarette with a burning tip. A sinister silence.*]

EVA: I know what it is.

FRED: What?

EVA: What ya got me in my stocking.

FRED: No.

EVA: It's a surprise.

FRED: No.

EVA: I like Christmas. Jesus was born. He likes me. Jesus loves all the little children. Want to know what I got you? It's easy to guess. You wear it on *this* finger. I'm saving it for Christmas. Like we said.

FRED: I never said.

EVA: You said you're my *fiancé*. Fred, my *fiancé*.

FRED: Don't say it like that.

EVA: I know you don't think you deserve me. But I won't let you throw away your one chance at happiness. There's not many chances people get. I'm your one and only chance. You think life is nothing but sorrow, and misery is a blessing from God. But you deserve happiness, you deserve me. I got my shoes dyed bone ivory to match the bridal dress. We might as well think about having children. Some kids would be nice.

FRED: It's not going to work out like everybody hoped.

EVA: It's going to work out like I hoped. Right after Christmas we're going to the justice of the peace and tying the knot.

FRED: Eva, I didn't wanna bother you with this and cause you to have a nervous breakdown.

EVA: What?

FRED: There's a muscular constriction. My heart's hard. It's not pumping as much blood as it should. It'll kill me. Two or three months. Could be days. The heart is a muscle and mine is decayed.

EVA: I don't believe you have such a heart like that. A decayed heart.

FRED: It's the way it is with my heart.

[FRED *and* EVA *look at each other steadily.*]

I won't make a widow out of you. Wouldn't be right. I can't let a young woman marry a terminal man. God would strike me down for selfish pride. You don't wanna make me look bad in the eyes of the Lord? Would you?

EVA: No. Not that.

FRED: Not more of that. Keep me out of hell, Eva. The dentist is single.

EVA: He's married.

FRED: Separated. A long time. For good.

EVA: Maybe not.

FRED: Wife's filing for divorce. Got a big-time lawyer. She's serving papers after Christmas.

EVA: How do you know?

FRED: She let it slip after some scotch.

EVA: Fred, we're engaged.

FRED: That was before my heart's muscular constriction.

EVA: It's sworn between us.

FRED: Set your sights on the living.

EVA: Remember back in April? The filling-station lady?

FRED: Wasn't that a terrible tragic thing.

EVA: It sure was sad at the funeral visitation. Seeing her in a coffin. One of her kids, a little girl, was crawling up on the coffin like she never realized her mama was dead.

FRED: You already told me the whole story.

EVA: Everyone could see her underpants. Pink. The little girl's underpants. It was a funny sight.

FRED: "A funny sight."

EVA: Her daddy had to carry her off that corpse. Crying all the way. He was the widower. Manager of the Texaco station. To his everlasting regret he was not there the night his wife got shot and killed.

FRED: You'll get the money. The running-away money. I won't need it dead.

EVA: When do I get it?

FRED: I'll give it to you on Christmas. In a wrapped package.

EVA: How much of it do I get?

FRED: Pretty much all.

EVA: Your heart's fine.

FRED: I don't lie.

EVA: That's not true. Both of us . . . You know I lie. On the Bible and under God. Tell me for real about your heart.

FRED: I'm dying, Eva! You like hearing it? I'll say it again. I am a dead man. Terminal. A corpse.

EVA: You're scaring me.

FRED: Boo!

EVA: I've been waiting. Here waiting for everything to be that is not going to be.

FRED I'm the one who is dying.

EVA: At least you're going somewhere.

[EVA *exits as* FRED *draws on the cigarette and lights come up on* BILL PERCH's *motel room.*]

SCENE 2: ROSY BRINGS A CHRISTMAS TREE TO THE MOTEL

[BILL PERCH's *motel room at the Jacksonian Motel. Time: the night of the murder—December 17, 1964.* PERCH *stands by the bed wearing a suit and tie. He clips his fingernails carefully with nail scissors. Silence. He goes to the phone and picks up the receiver. He dials the rotary phone and waits while it rings.*]

PERCH: Hello, Mama . . . We're doing fine. How're you? . . . Not a thing to worry about. It's a lull, a lull is circular, it's round, in the end it's not a lull . . . I don't know, it could be people are taking better care of their teeth, fluoride, dental floss. It's never one thing; it's an amalgam, to use a dental analogy . . . Uh huh, I know. The fact is, unfortunately, we can't come Christmas Day, Susan doesn't want to make the drive. She wants to stay home. Have Christmas at home . . . Tell Daddy I'll come hunt with him on the weekend . . . Mama, I do not need any more of your unsolicited advice. You don't seem to take it into consideration that I'm a member of the American Dental Association, I've given the lieutenant governor Novocain. I am not getting "huffy" . . . Yes, I deposited the check. Tell Daddy I won't need any more. Things will start up after the first of the year. It's just a—

[*Knocking is heard at the door.*]

—lull. Someone's knocking at the door . . . I don't know who, I have to go see . . . Susan's here. She's in the bathroom . . . Mama, people go to the goddamn bathroom . . .

[*Knocking, now more hesitant, is heard again.*]

I'm not being rude. There's someone knocking at the door. Mama, I have to go answer my front door.

[PERCH *hangs up the phone and goes to answer the door.* ROSY *stands at the door holding a small Christmas tree and a box of ornaments.* ROSY *is a strange girl with acne on her face. She wears a coat that she does not take off.*]

Rosy.

ROSY: Hi.

PERCH: What's that?

ROSY: A Christmas tree.

PERCH: Where's your mother?

ROSY: She left. She'll come back to pick me up.

PERCH: Where'd she go?

ROSY: I don't know. She wants me to decorate this tree with you.

PERCH: I don't want a tree in here.

ROSY: Yes, sir.

[ROSY *moves to take the tree away.*]

PERCH: Bring it in. We don't want to upset your mother.

[ROSY *brings in the tree.*]

Your mother is crazy. You know that?

ROSY: Yes, sir.

PERCH: When is she coming back?

ROSY: She said she wanted us to decorate the tree and have supper in the restaurant.

PERCH: I'll buy you a steak. A filet.

ROSY: I just want the fish sticks.

PERCH: You need to eat a substantial meal. A filet or T-bone steak. Something to work your jaw.

ROSY: Yes, sir. [*About the ornaments*] Should I put these on?

PERCH: Yes. Let's not upset your mother.

[ROSY *starts to put ornaments on the tree.*]

What do you want for Christmas?

ROSY: A wicker wheelchair. I saw one in an antique store on Capitol Street. If I got it I wouldn't have to walk. I could just roll around.

PERCH: I'm not getting you a goddamn wheelchair.

ROSY: Yes, sir.

PERCH: Did you try out for the Murrah Misses drill team?

ROSY: They didn't pick me. I didn't try my hardest so they didn't pick me.

PERCH: Always try your hardest.

ROSY: Yes, sir. I just didn't this once.

PERCH: You won't get anywhere unless you try your hardest, even then you could end up in a ditch like your Uncle Jim. He just drove off the road and it was over. Don't speed on roads that curve.

ROSY: I won't. I didn't get my driver's license. I failed the test.

PERCH: You failed the test?

ROSY: Yes, sir.

PERCH: Why?

ROSY: I couldn't parallel park.

PERCH: Didn't your mother teach you?

ROSY: She doesn't know how.

PERCH: I'll teach you. We'll go out to the parking lot at the football coliseum and I'll teach you. We'll go some Sunday when it's empty.

ROSY: Yes, sir.

PERCH [*about an ornament*]: What's that?

ROSY: The glass slipper.

PERCH: Don't put it on this tree. It's your mother's favorite. Put it on the tree at home. I'll see it there.

ROSY: Mama says you won't listen to her.

PERCH: I listen to your mother.

ROSY: She says I need to be the go-between and tell you she doesn't want you to come home for Christmas.

[*Slight but sharply painful beat.*]

PERCH: You want me, don't you?

ROSY: Yes, sir.

PERCH: I found a psychiatrist in New Orleans to take your mother to. No one here would ever know that we went. You could come with us and help explain your mother's problems. Tell how she threw hot coffee and locks herself in the bathroom. Sits in the tub all day without water. I need a witness. Would you do that? Be my witness? Your mother likes to lie. I don't want to put you on the spot. Your skin's broken out. That happens in adolescence. Open your mouth. Smile. Those teeth are good. You have good teeth.

ROSY: Yes, sir.

PERCH: Let's get some supper. Go wash your hands. You can have a Shirley Temple and a Baked Alaska.

ROSY: Yes, sir.

[ROSY *goes into the bathroom and washes her hands. There is the sound of rushing water.*]

PERCH: Did you bring your toothbrush?

ROSY [*offstage*]: Yes, sir.

PERCH: I want you to brush after every meal.

[ROSY *enters from the bathroom.*]

ROSY: I do.

PERCH: Better wash my hands. And we'll go.

[PERCH *exits to the bathroom. There is the sound of rushing water.* ROSY *looks at the small Christmas tree for a moment, then turns to the audience. The end of scene 2 flows directly into scene 3.*]

SCENE 3: PERCH MEETS FRED AND EVA

[*In the Jacksonian bar/restaurant. Time: May 1964, afternoon.* FRED *is behind the bar.* ROSY *steps through space and speaks to the audience.*]

ROSY: The separation. My parents' separation.

It was a temporary measure. A limited arrangement.

May.

My father moved out of our house in May. My birthday month. I turned sixteen. It was after my parents fought and he hurt her— worse than always.

[PERCH *enters and goes to sit at the bar.*]

Daddy moved to the Jacksonian Motel. Just for a time. A short time. A temporary measure.

[ROSY *exits.* PERCH *is drinking a scotch.*]

FRED: Another drink?

PERCH: Well . . .

[*He downs his drink.*]

Good timing.

FRED: My peripheral vision is keen.

PERCH: Nice to hear a man speak up for himself. Don't bury it with false pride.

FRED: I can sense what people want.

PERCH: Give people what they want, in case they've forgotten.

FRED [*giving* PERCH *a drink*]: Nice smile. Many men don't have nice smiles. You have got one.

PERCH: I'm a dentist.

FRED: I'm impressed.

PERCH: Dr. Bill Perch.

FRED: Fred Weber.

PERCH: Do you take care of your teeth, Fred?

FRED: My teeth are very important to me.

PERCH: Many people don't realize the correlation between oral conditions and general health. To say it is profound is not to overstate it. If you would like to make an appointment, I have a business card.

FRED: Alright.

PERCH: I don't like to advertise myself but will not stand on false pride concerning your teeth.

FRED [*looking at the card*]: You work here in Jackson?

PERCH: Medical Arts Building on North State Street.

FRED: How long are you visiting us?

PERCH: Not long . . . A day or two here in May.

FRED: May's a pretty month.

PERCH: I'm known as the Painless Dentist. Come to me and you'll feel
no pain. It's not like the old days. There's a whole new era of steril-
ity. I use disposable needles. X-ray machines are much improved. I
have the high-speed drills with water coolant, not the belt-driven.
Reclining motorized dental chair. Music. I let patients select the
radio channel they prefer. It gives them a sense of ease and distrac-
tion. Much of it is in the manner. You hypnotize the fear with a
steady manner. Of course I do use anesthesia when needed. Many
options there, Fred: nitrous oxide, Novocain, lidocaine, sodium
pentothal, chloroform. I can fix it to where you don't feel a thing.

FRED: I'll make an appointment.

PERCH: We all need regular oral examinations.

[*At the ice machine.* EVA *enters dressed in her finest. She opens the
heavy lid. She picks up a piece of ice and rubs her forehead and wrists.*]

EVA: Dear Jesus. Forgive me, Jesus. Forgive me for everything I swore
on that courtroom Bible.

[EVA *slams down the lid of the ice machine.*]

[*In the bar/restaurant.* FRED *gives* PERCH *a fresh drink.*]

PERCH: I usually don't. I'm very disciplined. But this morning's paper—
nothing to make you turn down a drink.

FRED: Yeah.

PERCH: The Negro church in Meridian.

FRED: What?

PERCH: Another fire bomb.

FRED: Had not heard.

PERCH: Third one this month.

[EVA *enters.*]

EVA: Fred, I'm back.

[FRED *goes to her.*]

FRED: How'd it go?

EVA: Good. They recorded me on a machine. All the lawyers were there, pro and con and prosecution. I swore to them every detail and they believed me. I want to buy a sensible wedding dress. Not like in the fairy tales. I'm not sixteen. I never was sixteen.

FRED: Eva.

EVA: I like it when you say my name.

FRED: Eva. Eva?

EVA: Yeah?

FRED: I have to take the ring back. I borrowed it from a friend and it has to be returned.

EVA: I know.

FRED: Here's a drink.

EVA: Thanks. [*About the ring*] It looks good on me. Could I keep it for tonight?

FRED: No.

EVA: It's still true though. It's in the public record. We're engaged. You're my fiancé. That's what I said in the room on the recording machine. I swore it on a courtroom Bible.

FRED: Eva, the ring.

EVA: Will you get me another?

FRED: I told you I would.

EVA: Swear on a stack of Bibles?

FRED: I swear on every Bible there is in creation.

[EVA *hands* FRED *the ring.*]

EVA: Get me one just like this.

FRED: Won't be no comparison.

[FRED *exits with the ring.*]

EVA: He's so sweet. We're engaged. Fred is my fiancé. I was just downtown giving alibi evidence against the colored man who killed the cashier lady at the Texaco. Don't you think he should be lynched?

PERCH: I do not.

EVA: He will be.

PERCH: The man hasn't been arraigned.

EVA: He'll be found guilty and sentenced to execution.

PERCH: There's no evidence I know of.

EVA: The paper says he's the prime suspect 'cause he worked right there on the premises.

PERCH: I use that Texaco station. Louis Wright is seventy something years old, has glaucoma.

EVA: He was the only colored employed at the station. And he knew the system.

PERCH: I think folks need to stop jumping to conclusions and wait for some actual facts.

EVA: Are you some sort of outside agitator?

PERCH: No, ma'am.

EVA: Where're you from?

PERCH: Here. Jackson.

EVA: Where in Jackson?

PERCH: In Eastover.

EVA [*impressed*]: You have a house in Eastover?

PERCH: Yes, ma'am.

EVA: That's a real wealthy area. Big fancy houses and yards. What's your occupation?

PERCH: I'm a dentist.

EVA: A dentist? You don't mind putting your fingers in people's mouths? Touching their tongues?

PERCH: You grow accustomed to it. Easily.

EVA: I wouldn't. All the slobber and blood and you could get bit. You need strong hands to be a dentist. Yours look strong. Look at the hair on your knuckles. Wouldn't want that tickling in my mouth.

PERCH: You'd be surprised how painless a trip to the dentist can be.

EVA: I don't think I would. You know why? 'Cause I don't even have a dentist. My mouth is sweet. Naturally kissable. I see you're married. Maybe you can help Fred pick out my ring. Introduce him to a fine jeweler.

PERCH: I don't know a lot about jewelry. My specialties are gum disease and anesthesia.

EVA: Why are you staying here? At the Jacksonian if you live in Eastover?

PERCH: We're painting our house. We're having the house painted.

EVA: What color?

[PERCH *shrugs his shoulders in a distracted manner.*]

Don't you know? Bet your wife knows.

PERCH: Yes. Susan. I have a wife, Susan.

EVA: Any kids?

PERCH: A daughter.

EVA: Where are they?

PERCH: Shopping.

EVA: All women like to shop. Especially if they have money. To get pretty things.

PERCH: Alright. Very nice talking to you.

EVA: Does that mean you're going?

PERCH: I need to retire to my room.

EVA: It's early. It's afternoon.

PERCH: Yes, I believe it is. Good day, Miss . . .

EVA: White. Eva White.

PERCH: Dr. Bill Perch.

EVA: The dentist.

PERCH: Yes, ma'am.

[PERCH *exits.* EVA *raises her hand and gazes at her ring finger.*]

SCENE 4: SUSAN ARRIVES AT THE JACKSONIAN

[*In the bar/restaurant. Time: the night of the murder—December 17, 1964.* ROSY *sits alone at a table picking at her Baked Alaska.* FRED *wipes off the bar.*]

FRED: Are you enjoying your Baked Alaska?

ROSY: It's big.

[PERCH *enters. He is returning from the bathroom.*]

PERCH [*to* ROSY]: What time did your mother say she was coming back?

ROSY: She didn't tell me.

PERCH: I don't understand people who cannot grasp time. The importance of time. Go on and finish your dessert.

ROSY: Yes, sir.

PERCH: My wife does not adhere to time. She doesn't see that things can only happen in time. Without time where are we? I'll look for her car—out on the highway.

[PERCH *exits.* FRED *walks to* ROSY's *table and points at the Baked Alaska.* EVA *enters and watches* FRED.]

FRED: You don't want to finish it?

ROSY: No.

FRED: I'll take it.

[FRED *takes the Baked Alaska.* EVA *sits down at* ROSY'S *table.*]

EVA: What do you think about Fred? Have you looked at him?

ROSY: Yeah.

EVA: Does he look sick to you? Like he's on death's door?

ROSY: Don't know.

EVA: I don't wanna marry a dead man. I have my dreams. You want to see my shoes? They match the bridal dress.

ROSY: I saw them. You showed me.

[FRED *exits behind the bar.*]

EVA: Where's your homework?

ROSY: I'm out of school for Christmas.

EVA: I'm glad I don't go to school now. With them.

ROSY: You mean Negroes?

EVA: How many you got all together?

ROSY: Five.

EVA: Five. I never had any, they didn't let 'em in.

ROSY: I got two in English and three in P.E.

EVA: How many Jews?

ROSY: Don't know.

EVA: Good thing you're doing it and not me.

ROSY: Did you ever even finish high school?

EVA [*lying*]: Yeah. I did.

ROSY: What year?

EVA: When are your parents divorcing?

ROSY: My parents don't believe in divorce.

EVA: Your daddy's been living here at the Jacksonian since May. He's our longest staying customer.

ROSY: My parents will never divorce. People who are nice don't do that. Only trashy people do that, or movie stars who are rich trashy people.

EVA: Takes care of his own laundry. His shirts. Underwear and shirts. I never knew a married man to do his own laundry.

ROSY: Everything in our family is fine.

[FRED *enters.*]

EVA: Fred has me an engagement ring for my Christmas stocking. But I can't afford a funeral. I look old in black.

ROSY: Eva.

EVA: What?

ROSY: No one is ever going to marry you.

EVA: Why do you say that? What is wrong with you? It's not true. I'm getting married. If it's not Fred it will be another man. One who is right close by.

ROSY: My daddy is never going to associate with you in real society.

EVA: You got no idea about grown-up behavior. They will fool you every time.

ROSY: It would be beneath him.

[PERCH *enters.* FRED *serves him a scotch.*]

PERCH: Yes, sir, Fred, your peripheral vision is keen.

FRED: Why, thank you, Dr. Perch.

EVA: What are those things on your face?

ROSY: Nothing.

EVA: Red pus-y things? Makes you look uglier than you are.

ROSY: Good.

EVA: Why would you want to be ugly?

ROSY: For the good of humankind.

EVA: What do you mean?

ROSY: Other people can help themselves to feeling better than me. Knowing they don't have a face like mine makes them smirk and sigh with relief. I don't want to clear these up; I prefer to keep them aflame. For humanity.

EVA: If you was my stepdaughter, I'd thrash you with rawhide till you washed that face.

ROSY: Hardy, har, har.

[SUSAN *enters. She brings Christmas gifts. Apples covered with cloves, decorated with cinnamon sticks and velvet ribbon. They are uniquely beautiful.*]

SUSAN: Merry Christmas! Merry Chrissy!

PERCH: Susan!

SUSAN: I've brought y'all presents. Here, Eva, just a little happy. And here's one for you, Fred.

FRED: Thanks.

EVA: Yeah.

SUSAN: Homemade Christmas sachet. Rosy and I pressed hundreds of cloves into each apple, one by one by one till all our fingers were worn out and blistered. The cinnamon sticks and velvet ribbons remind me of an old-fashioned Christmas.

PERCH: Rosy had dinner. A T-bone steak. I made her eat it without ketchup.

SUSAN: Did she have steak sauce?

PERCH: Only a dab. Right, Rosy?

ROSY: Yes, sir.

PERCH: It was a good meal. T-bone is a fine cut of beef. Tell your mother.

ROSY: It was good.

SUSAN: She hardly eats anything I cook.

ROSY: Yes I do.

PERCH: Don't contradict your mother.

ROSY: Yes, sir.

PERCH: We don't have to go to Mama's and Daddy's for Christmas.

SUSAN: They love to see you. I bought gifts you can take from us. A negligee for your mother and an engraved sterling ashtray for your father. Did you get your Christmas tree?

PERCH: Yes.

SUSAN: Good. Did you decorate it?

PERCH: Looks good. You want to come see it?

SUSAN: Well, alright. Rosy?

PERCH: She already saw it.

SUSAN: She can see it again.

PERCH: Rosy, do you want to see the tree again?

ROSY: I don't know. No.

PERCH: Alright. Let's go see it.

[PERCH *and* SUSAN *exit.*]

FRED [*to* EVA]: You need to clean Three and Seven. Carla went home. Swollen kneecaps. Like somebody hit her with a baseball bat.

EVA: She's just lazy.

FRED: Go on.

EVA: Later I'll go on. [*To* ROSY, *who is holding the baby Jesus figure from the manger scene*] Don't touch that. Don't play with his swaddling. That's Christ Baby Jesus, not a doll! Put him back.

ROSY: You put him back. I have to brush my teeth.

[ROSY *exits to the bathroom with her purse.*]

EVA: I know what is going on here. I can smell it burning. You don't want to marry me and you're making up lies. Just remember, they have not gassed that nigger for killing the Texaco woman; so don't try to pull one. Not on me. I will go to jail for perjury to get you gassed.

FRED: Do you know who you are talking to, Eva? You are talking to a murderer. And I have few qualms left. Really no qualms. Whatsoever.

EVA: I'll go to the dentist. I'll go entangle him but understand you are the one I love but for hating you entirely.

[EVA *exits.*]

[*In the motel room.* SUSAN *and* PERCH *enter.* SUSAN *looks at the forlorn tree. She goes to it.* PERCH *watches as* SUSAN *rearranges ornaments on the tree. She has a good eye and improves the look of the tree.*]

[*In the bar/restaurant.* ROSY *enters from the bathroom wearing dark lipstick.*]

FRED: Did you put on lipstick?

ROSY: No.

FRED: Would you like another Cherry Coke?

ROSY: Yeah. Why not.

FRED: I like you so I'll add extra cherries.

ROSY: Fred?

FRED: Yeah?

ROSY: Are you dying?

FRED: No. That's a lie to get her out of my hair. I can't marry Eva. She smells like broken-up crayons in a dirty room.

ROSY: Yeah. All the colors you don't want to use.

SCENE 5: SUSAN VISITS PERCH'S MOTEL ROOM

[*In the motel room. Time: the night of the murder—December 17, 1964. With* PERCH *next to her,* SUSAN *stands back and appraises the tree.*]

SUSAN: It needs lights. Lights make the tree. I'll send Rosy with some lights.

PERCH: I don't need lights. Anyway . . . Coming home. I've been at the Jacksonian for a time. Need to take charge of my family. Be with my family.

SUSAN: No.

PERCH: There is a psychiatrist in New Orleans we could go see.

SUSAN: What for?

PERCH: I need you to understand everything isn't all my fault.

SUSAN: I think it is.

PERCH: All my fault? Susan, you have moods. You swear at me and threaten. Get hysterical.

SUSAN: There are medical reasons for that. They take things out of you and you are not the same. You're different. Very changed. There's no money in my checking account.

PERCH: I'm working on that.

SUSAN: I had an ovarian cyst. The size of a pea the doctor told me. I went under anesthesia and you let them take out every woman part of me!

PERCH: It was a medical necessity, Dr. Carpenter—Susan, you're getting—don't get—

SUSAN [*overlapping*]: I would never have given consent! They gutted me! You let them cut out my womb. You let them do it! You son of a bitch! I could kill you!

[SUSAN *claws him deep and hard on the face.* PERCH *feels the marks on his face.* SUSAN *holds her hand, looking at the flesh that is under her nails.*]

PERCH: For God's sake. Susan. Please. Dr. Carpenter advised—

[SUSAN *goes into the bathroom.*]

My God. I didn't want to lose you. I'm sorry. My God. I'm sorry. My God.

[SUSAN *returns with a wet towel and gives it to* PERCH *to soothe his face.*]

SUSAN: Bill. Here.

PERCH: I don't know. Things keep going downhill. I try to stop them but they keep sliding and . . .

SUSAN: What?

PERCH: In the end things will be okay. It's a lull.

[*A silence.* SUSAN *turns away.* PERCH *looks at her. She breathes. He breathes.*]

SUSAN: I took an arrangement of cauliflowers and irises to the garden club. I thought it was revolutionary. But it went unappreciated and was mocked.

PERCH: I think it's because you're an artist. You have artistic feelings.

SUSAN: I'm not an artist. I'm a wife and mother. I'm nothing. A nonentity.

PERCH: Everyone thinks . . . you're a lovely lady.

SUSAN: People talk about me behind my back. I don't tell them but they know you're living here. They know you hit me.

PERCH: I never would. Never again.

SUSAN: I can't kill myself. I would never kill myself. If I did it wouldn't be in a violent fashion. Not a gun or wrists cut; cut wrists. No blood. Blood is private. It would never be at home. Not where Rosy could find me. I'd come here to the Jacksonian, bring pills and gin. That would be the way. To float away. With a nice brand of gin, morphine, Novocain, ether. I could get it. I could borrow it from you. But I never would kill myself, no matter how good of an idea I thought it was, because even if I did, nothing would change. Nothing would be lost or gained even by that. My nose is all wrong.

PERCH: No, it isn't.

SUSAN: They have surgery now. Surgery that could give me a classical nose.

PERCH: You don't need surgery.

SUSAN: Clearly, clearly, clearly I do.

PERCH: Susan, I want to try.

SUSAN: I know you do. This place is depressing. The carpet is the color of despair. You should look for a nice apartment. I keep telling you that.

PERCH: I like it here because it's temporary. And we came here one time together before we were married.

SUSAN: I remember.

PERCH: Same time of year.

SUSAN: It was at my instigation. I didn't want to be a virgin on my wedding day. I thought it was sappy—a virgin bride.

PERCH: You came disguised as something. Incognito.

SUSAN: I wore a hat with a veil so I wouldn't be recognized. I turned my engagement ring around to make it look like a wedding band.

PERCH: You were the most beautiful girl in the world.

SUSAN: I thought no one was ever going to marry me because my nose was all wrong. But you did not seem to mind it. You saw other things.

PERCH: All along, I wanted you. Susan Stanford. I only wanted you.

SUSAN: You brought me here and I demurred. Clinging to a worn-out innocence. I was a virgin until the day I got married. What a silly thing.

PERCH: It wasn't silly.

SUSAN: You were gallant.

PERCH: I wanted to do what you wanted.

SUSAN: You did.

PERCH: Good.

SUSAN: I let you feel under my skirt. You're a dentist. Your hands are always clean. Your fingers are agile. They understand how to manipulate with precision in small cavities.

PERCH: Let me touch you there. I want to. Pretty girl.

SUSAN: Rosy is waiting.

PERCH: She likes it here. She's made friends. Pretty, pretty girl.

SUSAN: I need a scotch. With ice.

PERCH: I'll get ice.

[PERCH *exits.* SUSAN *smells the perfume on the pulse of her wrist.* ROSY *appears on stage wearing her coat and holding schoolbooks. She goes to* SUSAN *and smells her perfume.*]

ROSY: Ice, blood, ice.

Rosy is waiting. She likes it here. She's made friends.

October. *Tu es un cochon.* I have to study French.

[ROSY *leaves the motel room and steps through time into the bar/restaurant. She sits at a table and opens one of her books.* SUSAN *exits.*]

SCENE 6: ROSY AND FRED HAVE A STRANGE ENCOUNTER

[*In the bar/restaurant. Time: October 1964.* ROSY *sits at a table wearing her coat. A schoolbook is laid in front of her. She holds a pencil and stares out at nothing.*]

[*At the ice machine.* FRED *appears, smoking. Something is disturbing him. He fills a silver ice bucket and walks into the bar/restaurant.*]

FRED: Rosy. Where's your daddy?

ROSY: Gone. Mama's late.

FRED: Aren't you hot in that coat?

ROSY: I don't know.

FRED: You don't know? Why not?

ROSY: I can't tell if it's hot or cold. I don't feel the weather.

FRED: It's warm. For October.

ROSY: I don't feel weather.

FRED: Want a Cherry Coke? On the house?

ROSY: No.

FRED: Are you wearing lipstick?

[ROSY *is not.*]

ROSY: No.

FRED: Looks like you are. Pretty lips. Rosy.

ROSY: I have to study.

FRED: What are you studying?

ROSY: French.

FRED: I don't know French.

ROSY [*not necessarily to him*]: Tu es un cochon.

FRED: What's that?

ROSY: It means, you are a pig.

FRED: Me? No. Why me?

ROSY: What you did. To that woman. You know.

FRED: I know I'm not a pig. You don't like me. Do you? You don't call me "Sir." Most of the girls, the ladies, find me to be a man with appeal. But you don't see the allure. That's why I like you, Rosy. That is why I am drawn to you. You're a good judge of character. You see deep into the pit of the human soul. And that is how I look at you. I see how pretty you are both inside and out. You are pulsing with sweetness. Inside and out. You know what I mean?

[ROSY *starts writing with the pencil, ignoring him.*]

I got something I can do most people can't. I swallow swords. I am a sword swallower. Not a fake trick. The real feat.

[ROSY *stops writing and looks at him.*]

ROSY: How's it feel?

FRED: It never feels pleasant or comfortable. You have to learn to relax muscles that are not under your voluntary control. Learning to ignore an involuntary reaction to a natural bodily function takes a tremendous amount of will and practice. Over and over. Deliberately activating the gag reflex. Over and over. Causing vomiting, choking, gagging.

ROSY: That's sickening.

FRED: Yeah, but eventually you are able to remove a natural and involuntary process that protects you from harm.

ROSY: Why would ya?

FRED: Glory! Southern defiance pride and glory. It's the most dangerous job in the world. Swallowing steel.

ROSY: What's the longest sword you ever swallowed?

FRED: Twenty-nine-inch solid-steel blade. Thirty-three inches is the world record.

ROSY [*holding up a stainless-steel knife*]: Swallow this.

FRED: That's cutlery.

ROSY: It's not long. It's short. Should be easy.

FRED: Thing is, Rosy, I had to give up the practice of sword swallowing. Lacerated some blood vessels in the trachea. Blood shot out of my mouth in a gush. A ruby fountain. That was my final performance.

ROSY: You made it up.

FRED: No. I would not lie to you. I would not.

ROSY: I have to study French.

FRED: Take off your coat.

ROSY: I'm not hot. I don't feel weather.

FRED: Watch me.

[ROSY *looks at him.* FRED *drinks a glass of water.*]

Watch what I do.

[FRED *takes the stainless-steel knife and thrusts it down his throat.* FRED *gags and coughs. He pulls out the knife. The blade has blood on it.* FRED *is still choking.* ROSY *stands up.*]

ROSY: Are you hurt?

FRED [*still coughing*]: I did that for you 'cause I think you're pretty. Inside and out.

ROSY: Don't do that for me.

FRED: You've cast a spell.

ROSY: I know you're no good.

FRED: But I am. I am good.

[ROSY *gathers her books.*]

ROSY: I'm sorry you bled. I'm leaving. I'll go wait for my mother. I'm sorry you bled. Don't bleed for me. Don't ever.

[ROSY *exits.* FRED *wipes the blood off his mouth.*]

SCENE 7: EVA LIES TO PERCH; SUSAN LEAVES

[*Flashback to the end of scene 5,* PERCH *and* SUSAN *in the motel room. Time: the night of the murder—December 17, 1964.*]

PERCH: Let me touch you there. I want to. Pretty girl.

SUSAN: Rosy is waiting.

PERCH: She likes it here. She's made friends. Pretty, pretty girl.

SUSAN: I need a scotch. With ice.

PERCH: I'll get ice.

[PERCH *exits.* SUSAN *smells the perfume on the pulse of her wrist.*]

[*At the ice machine. Time: the night of the murder—December 17, 1964.* EVA *stands at the ice machine drinking a Coke.* PERCH *enters carrying a metal ice bucket.*]

EVA: Hi.

PERCH: Miss Eva.

EVA: I was just changing some bedsheets.

PERCH: Uh huh.

EVA: You need yours changed?

PERCH: They're fine.

EVA: Haven't been wrinkled?

PERCH: No. Not yet.

EVA: All clean?

[PERCH *scoops ice into the bucket.*]

How are things with your wife?

PERCH: Fine.

EVA: Do you expect to get back with her?

PERCH: If she will have me.

EVA: I think she won't.

PERCH: Why not?

EVA: I heard—

PERCH: What?

[EVA *takes a piece of ice from his bucket and sensually glides it across her mouth.*]

EVA: Different things, on different occasions. Over periods of time.

PERCH: Such as?

EVA: Mrs. Perch is filing divorce papers on you.

PERCH: Who said?

EVA: Rosy.

PERCH: Rosy?

EVA: She thought you knew.

PERCH: No. I did not know.

EVA: You need fresh towels? I could give you extra.

[PERCH *walks away with the ice.* EVA *slings the ice cube back into the ice machine. She exits.*]

[*In the motel room.* SUSAN *sits on the edge of the bed charged with sensuality.* PERCH *enters with the ice.*]

PERCH: Ice.

SUSAN: Yes.

[PERCH *puts ice in a glass and pours in the scotch. He hands her a glass.*]

Thank you.

[SUSAN *takes a sip and looks at him with flirtatious nervousness.*]

I don't think I should stay. I feel . . . Maybe I should go? How silly. I'm demurring once again.

PERCH: Alright. Have your drink and go home.

SUSAN: Well. Merry Christmas.

PERCH: I've thought it over. Given it thought. I'm better off here. I can't make it work. The marriage. I'm not made for marriage. That is the bold and naked truth.

SUSAN: You told me it would work out.

PERCH: I had that wrong.

SUSAN: You fooled me.

PERCH: Fooled myself.

SUSAN: What are we going to do?

PERCH: Aren't you filing for divorce?

[*A moment between them.*]

SUSAN: I spoke with an attorney.

PERCH: What attorney?

SUSAN: Tom Royals.

PERCH: Tom Royals. He's first-rate. So what all did you tell Tom Royals about me? About our lives?

SUSAN: Nothing. I just wanted some information.

PERCH: What information?

SUSAN: He said you'd have to support us. Provide for us.

PERCH: Haven't I done that? Christ, I've always provided for my family! You don't have to go to Tom Royals to find that out! Did you file papers? Huh?

SUSAN: . . .

PERCH: I believed things could work out but they can't.

SUSAN: Do you love me?

PERCH: Does it matter? It doesn't matter.

SUSAN: We're leaving. I'll get Rosy and we're going home.

PERCH: Tell Rosy Merry Christmas.

SUSAN: Son of a fucking bitch.

[SUSAN *exits.* PERCH *goes to a drawer, pulls out a brown bottle of morphine, and drinks from it. He exits into the bathroom.*]

[*In the bar/restaurant.* ROSY *is playing with the figures in the manger scene.* FRED *is smoking and watching her.* SUSAN *enters.*]

SUSAN: Rosy, we're leaving.

ROSY: Yes, ma'am.

SUSAN: I'm divorcing your father.

ROSY: Don't. She doesn't mean it. Please don't! Mama, please don't get divorced!

SUSAN: Poor Rosy. Poor Rosy. I hope sometimes she'll die young of something so she won't have to be in this world. It's not her world. It's a world some people do well in because somehow they imagine to think they are doing something, something, something. Climb a mountain because it's there. Kneel down and pray to a victim of torture nailed to a cross along with others. Not even on his own, along with others.

[SUSAN *hands* ROSY *her bag.*]

You drive. I can't drive.

ROSY: Please, don't get divorced! Mama, please don't! Please! I beg you, Mama! Please!

SUSAN [*overlapping with* ROSY]: STOP IT! STOP IT RIGHT NOW. ROSY, STOP!

ROSY: Yes, ma'am.

SUSAN: Please. Let's don't take ourselves so seriously.

[SUSAN *and* ROSY *exit.*]

[*In the motel room.* PERCH *enters from the bathroom with a tank of nitrous oxide and a mask. He inhales the gas. This is not his first hit. He laughs and reels around.*]

PERCH [*singing, perhaps*]: Rudolph too red nosed rain beer. Very shiny nose. Shiny red nose. Nose shiny red. Shiny, shiny. Nose. Red *all* red.

[EVA *knocks on the motel room door.*]

EVA: Dr. Perch?

PERCH: Miss Eva?

EVA: I brought you some extra towels.

PERCH: Whatever you got! Bring it in! I need it. Whatever you got.

[EVA *enters with towels. Aghast, she drops the towels.* ROSY *appears on stage wearing her coat. She addresses the audience.*]

ROSY: My parents did things they should not have done.

There were no reasons.

They say things happen for *reasons*. But the reasons are not real. It's just the swamp you're living on that *pulls* you under.

Under weeds, wet grass, mud. Lifetimes of rot and blood, lynched blood, buried in Mississippi soil.

How it pulls through the nerves in my mouth. I keep my mouth closed and push it back down.

September. Algebra. I'll try out for the drill team.

[*The sound of running water moves us from scene 7 to scene 8.*]

SCENE 8: EVA INADVERTENTLY REVEALS
FRED'S GUILT TO ROSY

[*In the motel room. Time: September 1964. The sound of running water continues.* PERCH *sits on the edge of the bed filing his nails. He talks to* ROSY, *who is brushing her teeth in the bathroom.*]

PERCH: Brush three minutes. Three full minutes on the clock.

ROSY [*offstage*]: Yes, sir.

PERCH: How do you like school so far?

ROSY [*offstage*]: Fine.

PERCH: What grade are you in?

ROSY [*offstage*]: Eleventh.

[PERCH *picks up a flier that is with* ROSY's *schoolbooks.*]

PERCH: You ought to try out for the drill team this year. The Murrah Misses. I'd come watch the game, see you at half-time.

ROSY [*offstage*]: Yes, sir.

[*Sound of water stops.* ROSY *enters from the bathroom with a toothbrush. She wears school clothes.*]

That was four minutes I brushed my teeth.

PERCH: Good. How's your mother?

ROSY: She says things are fine.

PERCH: Things are fine. Anybody asks you tell them things are fine.

ROSY: I do.

PERCH: Did she get the flowers I sent? The roses?

ROSY: Yes, sir.

PERCH: I send them every Monday so she'll have them for the week. I
   hope she likes them.

ROSY: She likes them.

PERCH: Your mother likes flowers. But she has difficulties. I know she'll
   come around. Things are going to be fine. You tell her I help you
   with your homework?

ROSY: Yes, sir. She's glad because she can't do algebra.

PERCH: Do you have any algebra for homework?

ROSY: Yes, sir.

[PERCH *takes the paper and studies it.*]

PERCH: I can help you. Hand me a pencil.

[ROSY *hands him a pencil. Throughout the following he writes answers
handily.*]

I always made good grades. That's why I could become a dentist.
A professional. My brother Jim could not cut it. Daddy always let
him know he had let him down. Mothers forgive your failures but
if you're a man's son, he sees you as a reflection. I've always looked
good in my father's eyes. Bright. Impressive. Jim did not make the
grade. Daddy tried but could not instill in him the simple principle
that privileges must be earned. "Every *right* must be *balanced* by
an accompanying *responsibility.*"

[ROSY *has heard this many times before and joins in with him on, "an
accompanying responsibility."*]

Maybe someday Jim would have been able to find his way. But he's gone now. We won't ever know about that. Have they got you in remedial math?

[PERCH *returns the completed page of algebra to* ROSY.]

ROSY: No, sir.

PERCH: How are your grades?

ROSY: Fine.

PERCH: Someday you'll be out of the ugly duckling phase.

ROSY: I know.

[EVA *knocks on the door.*]

EVA: I got the fan, Dr. Perch.

PERCH: Thank you, Miss Eva.

[EVA *enters with a fan.* ROSY *goes and sits on the bed.*]

Always feels like it will cool off in September. But it seems just to get hotter.

EVA: I'll set it up here.

PERCH: The heat does still.

EVA: Y'all hear the news?

PERCH: What news?

EVA: That old nigger got a stay of execution. Doesn't make sense to spare his life a day longer. They got the nigger that done it.

PERCH: What Negro?

EVA: The one robbed that Texaco station and shot the lady cashier. I never knew you could stay a nigger's execution.

PERCH: Negro.

EVA: Nigra.

PERCH: Knee-grow.

EVA: Doesn't matter what you call 'em. Ain't nothing gonna make 'em white.

PERCH: Well . . . it is hot. The heat does still.

[PERCH *heads for the door.*]

ROSY: Where are you going?

PERCH: Get something out of the car.

[PERCH *exits.*]

EVA: Your daddy's cute. Always so well groomed. Thing is the nigger's old and blind. Could die in the jail if they don't gas him fast. The law has *got* to stop monkeying around. Murder happened back in April. Now some Yankee's coming down here making appeals to the court. Got the law out hunting new evidence.

[EVA *plugs in the fan.*]

Running out investigating innocent white people out of prejudice, pure prejudice 'cause they sick of having all them coloreds filling up the jail. Want some white suspects for a change. Fred ought to be clear of all suspicion. He has an alibi. An airtight alibi.

ROSY: About what? What, Eva? What alibi?

[EVA *goes to* ROSY.]

EVA: They came here inquiring about his whereabouts concerning the night the cashier woman got robbed and killed. Some passerby saw a car looked like Fred's driving off after shots was heard. Got three numbers off the license plate that matched Fred's. Which was nothing but circumstantial coincident. Fred let them know he was nowhere near that situation. He was with me, his fiancée, and no one else. I swore to them it was all the truth. They took me in for questioning. Deposited me in front of a whole line of fancy rich men in suits with their secretaries. I had to tell the truth about me and Fred, what we were doing that night the cashier got shot. All of it was none of their business. It involved sexual relations. You might not know about that.

ROSY: I know what it is.

EVA: They didn't spare my modesty in any way. Everything. Every *detail*. Even told them that after the sexual relations I got up and went to the bathroom to douche out the seed. Did it three times for safety. I didn't like revealing that private information. I wanted people to believe I was a virgin. Pure and unsoiled till my wedding day. But the truth is the truth and God will forgive me. Every Sunday I ask Jesus to forgive me. Forgive me, Jesus, for every breath I take. He has to do it—forgive me. That's all He was born for. Every Sunday I get His forgiveness. Regular, like a bowel movement.

[EVA *gives* ROSY *a superior look.* ROSY *clutches her skin. A shudder runs through her.* EVA *turns the electric fan on high. It is loud and blows on her forcefully.*]

In the end they will execute that nigger in a gas chamber. All alone but with spectators. I'd like to see it. I'd look at him with pity. Christian pity. It wouldn't be hate.

ROSY: Oh Lord.

SCENE 9: THE DAY BILL PERCH DID SOMETHING BAD
TO HIS PATIENT, PHIL BOONE

[*In the bar/restaurant. Time: November 1964, afternoon.* FRED *is smoking behind the bar. The red tip of his cigarette burns.* SUSAN *enters.*]

SUSAN: Hello, Fred.

FRED: Nice to see you, Mrs. Perch. Scotch with ice.

SUSAN: Yes.

[*He gives her a drink.*]

Thank you. Have you seen Dr. Perch?

FRED: Not this day.

SUSAN: I called his room. He wasn't there. He's not at the office. Maybe he is somewhere off . . . doing something.

FRED: On a chore.

SUSAN: He's not coming home. I believe he's not.

FRED: You mean Dr. Perch?

SUSAN No, I don't know who I mean.

FRED: Oh. You looking forward to Thanksgiving, Mrs. Perch?

SUSAN: Yes. Are you?

FRED: Yes, ma'am.

SUSAN: Thinking about a turkey or a goose?

FRED: Goose.

SUSAN: I like your tattoo. Strawberries and a black snake. Where did you get it?

FRED: Gulfport.

SUSAN Are you from around here?

FRED: Yes, ma'am. Born and raised outside of Meridian. How about yourself?

SUSAN: I was born at St. Dominic's Hospital right here in Jackson.

FRED: I went away for a time. Went traveling. I was a performer for a time. But I came back here after all.

SUSAN: I'll end my days here. I don't want to, but I will.

FRED: Have you thought of going somewhere?

SUSAN: Nowhere to go. Where would I go? There's nowhere to go.

FRED: Some place.

SUSAN: Really, it's nice here. It's familiar.

FRED: Sure.

SUSAN: I'm happy to live in Mississippi. I hear outside this state, it's very different. People are not genuine.

FRED: This particular region has a lot to offer. Many good things.

SUSAN: The magnolia. The dogwoods.

FRED: This state invented the portable electric chair.

SUSAN: Really?

FRED: No other state had one. We were the first. Had it custom-built in Memphis. Folks were loath to give up hanging because it allowed the criminal to be executed right there in the place where he had committed his crime and been convicted. With the portable electric chair the tradition of geographical retribution could be maintained.

SUSAN: I see.

FRED: 'Course now we have the gas chamber. It's not portable. Stays up at the Parchman Penitentiary. There was a good deal of opposition from the people of Sunflower County. They did not want all the evil blood in the state spilled on their land alone.

SUSAN: I understand their reluctance. I'd feel the same.

FRED: Yes, ma'am.

SUSAN: But it must be more humane? Less painful? The gas chamber.

FRED: First fellow they put in was low-dosed. Took him forty-five ugly minutes to die. They try to prevent that now by testing the chamber on an animal before they bring in the man. Cats, rabbits. Could be a dog. Anything breathing.

SUSAN: My, you have quite a store of knowledge concerning our system of capital punishment.

FRED: It's a subject that interests me. I'm revealing myself to you. Do you mind?

SUSAN: No.

FRED: I think about it. I think even if they had the cyanide dose exactly correct, I'd rather be hung from a tree than die choking on poison strapped down in a box.

SUSAN: I hate living here. There's something in the humidity that makes me perspire drops of blood.

[She swirls her finger in the glass of melting ice.]

The water has melted. I mean the ice, the ice has melted. Water cannot melt. It evaporates or someone drinks it or bathes in it. Something happened with my husband. I heard it at the garden club. My husband loves his job more than anything else; he takes pride . . . He is a painless dentist. I'm not feeling well. Of all things. I'd better have my check.

FRED: I'll put it on your husband's room.

SUSAN: Very kind and gracious of you, Fred. The people here, in this state, they're kind. Why would anyone ever want to leave?

FRED: They don't.

[As SUSAN *stands to leave,* PERCH *enters disheveled. He is messed up on liquid morphine but maintaining.*]

PERCH: Susan, what are you doing here?

SUSAN: Having a drink.

PERCH: Would you like another? We'll have scotch. But he knows that. Fred's peripheral vision is keen. How are you?

SUSAN: Very well.

PERCH: Good. I hope it gets colder by Thanksgiving. I like a frost in the air.

[FRED *serves their drinks in silence.*]

SUSAN: Today I was at my garden club . . .

PERCH: Green thumb. Thumbs. Both of your thumbs are green.

SUSAN: I heard something awful.

PERCH: People are always running their mouths. It's nice to be a dentist. You don't have to listen to people going on and on. They can't talk with a drill down their throat.

SUSAN: No, no, no, no drill. Your patient, Phil Boone—nothing happened today, did it? This man, Phil Boone, his teeth? A patient you had today?

PERCH: Phil Boone? He's fine. Let me explain. I made an error in judgment. There need to be more precautions in dentistry. Some safeguards.

SUSAN: What safeguards?

PERCH: In the future, devices will be invented and errors will be a thing of the past. There may be accidents but not errors. No deliberate errors.

SUSAN: Bill, are you . . .

PERCH: What? Yes? Is there a question?

SUSAN: Could they take your license?

PERCH: My dental license? Where did you hear that? Dentistry is the meat and potatoes of my goddamn life.

SUSAN: I was concerned about our livelihood. How you would provide for us?

PERCH: I'll always provide for you. You're my wife.

SUSAN: I don't have anyone else but you.

PERCH: I know you don't.

SUSAN: You still have your parents. Both of them.

PERCH: Don't tell them about this.

SUSAN: I won't.

PERCH: They'd be upset for no reason. They only want me to succeed.

SUSAN: Well, you do. You always succeed. You always do. I feel whirly, of all things. I need to go home and lie down.

PERCH: I'll take you. Let me.

SUSAN: No. It's better when you are gone. Easier. A fresher smell all around. You need to stay here. At the Jacksonian.

[SUSAN *exits.*]

PERCH: I worry about her nature. She can be cruel. Say things no one could mean.

[PERCH *takes a brown bottle of morphine from his pocket.* FRED *brings* PERCH *a second scotch.* PERCH *displays the bottle of morphine to* FRED.]

Morpheus. God of oblivion.

[*He drinks from the bottle.*]

Susan had an operation. A hysterectomy. She blames me, even though Dr. Carpenter believed it was a necessity. I try to get along but there are times . . . I hit her. It may have been more than once. Most men in their right minds would not be able to stop themselves. They would not.

[ROSY *is revealed. She wears her coat unbuttoned.*]

ROSY: He's not coming home.

I believe he's not.

[FRED *exits.* PERCH *exits.*]

The swamp is rising to cover us all.

Another fire bomb in Meridian.

I don't let time go but it goes.

[He motms his mouth with his fingers.]

It pulls forward to the night of murder.

And I am released.

I want to get it over. Hurt me now, get it over.

Like Patsy Cline in the song.

[*Singing*] "If you got leavin' on your mind. Tell me now, get it over . . ."

SCENE 10: PERCH AND EVA GET INTO THE CHLOROFORM

[*In the motel room. Time: the night of the murder—December 17, 1964. Lights come up on* EVA *strutting around the room in her undergarments. She is lit on alcohol and cocaine.*]

EVA: Don't you just love people who have fun with their bodies? Those are the people you want to be with. People who love showing off because it's a whirlwind of pleasure.

[PERCH *enters from the bathroom carrying his medicine kit. His shirt is unbuttoned and his pants are falling down. Throbbing cocaine numbness has overtaken him.*]

All these things! You got these things! All these things!

[EVA *feels her breasts, ass, mouth, and crotch.*]

Don't hide! Don't hunch your shoulders! Have fun with your body! Look how it jiggles! Once I was nothing like this. I had to *learn*! I had to *learn* to be natural. They don't teach you that at school.

PERCH: No, they don't.

EVA: Hey.

PERCH: Yeah?

EVA: Fred is dying. Did you know Fred is dying?

PERCH: No.

EVA: I hope I live a *long* time. It's the only time I have not to be in hell. Would you marry me?

PERCH: I don't think I would. But could I do something to you?

EVA: What?

PERCH: I'd like to look inside your mouth. Put my hands into your mouth.

EVA: Why would you do that?

PERCH: I miss it.

EVA: What?

PERCH: The mouth.

EVA: Ain't you a dentist?

PERCH: Yes, I am. Let me see inside your mouth.

EVA: Only if you'll marry me.

PERCH: Alright, that's a deal.

EVA: Yeah! I'm getting married.

PERCH: Now stay still just a minute. Let me feel the lips. Upper, lower, vermilion border. Full of nerve endings, blood vessels, erogenous outside organ. Real strong, real flexible muscles.

[*He moves her mouth with his fingers.*]

Just a beautiful range of motion.

[*He lets go and talks to her in a soothing voice as he puts on a latex glove and removes dental tools from the medical kit.*]

Now please, Miss White, relax, please. There is nothing to be afraid of. This procedure will be completely painless. Now I'm going to need for you to open up your mouth. Wider, please. Wider. Good.

[EVA *opens her mouth wide.* PERCH *feels inside her mouth.*]

Fine-looking tongue. Grand whale of the mouth. Powerful muscles—able to emerge and reemerge into this phantasmagorical maw—the mouth. Wider. That's good. Here they are, the beauties, the teeth. Every one has a mind of its own. A particular design and function. Grind, pierce, cut, chew. Tear.

[*He moves her jaw with his hand.*]

You have a slight malocclusion.

EVA: What?

PERCH: The teeth in your upper and lower jaw don't meet properly.

EVA: My teeth meet properly.

PERCH: I could fix it for you.

EVA: No!

[EVA *pours herself a scotch.*]

PERCH: Painlessly. With anesthesia. An-esthesia, an-esthesia. A Greek word. "An" for without. "Esthesia" for sensibility. Without sensibility. Wouldn't you like that? To be without sensibility?

EVA: I don't even have a dentist.

[PERCH *snorts cocaine.*]

PERCH: I'm a terrific dentist. Painless. I like to make people smile. My own daddy won't smile. Has bad teeth, terrible gums, severe halitosis which leads to social awkwardness. I've implored him but he won't let me touch his teeth. Gingivitis has spread to the supporting structures, causing irreparable damage to his mouth. He's a good man, my father. Tried to instill values in me and my brother. He always told us, "*Every* right must be *balanced* by an accompanying *responsibility*."

EVA: Oh yeah! Yeah, yeah. "With rare exceptions people of other backgrounds simply cannot comprehend the Anglo-Saxon principle of Equal Justice Under The Law and the fact that *every* right must be *balanced* by an accompanying *responsibility*." "Get out your Bible and pray! You will hear from us!" That's another part of the leaflet.

PERCH: What leaflet?

EVA: The one for the KKK.

PERCH: What my daddy said—what he said, wasn't from any goddamn leaflet. It's an aphorism. An original aphorism.

EVA: No, it's from the KKK leaflet.

PERCH: You don't know basically shit, Eva.

[EVA *makes a K sound and mimes shooting a machine gun.*]

EVA: K-K-K-K!

[PERCH *opens a drawer and retrieves a brown bottle of morphine. He drinks from the bottle.* EVA *pulls him toward her.*]

I got a good memory for things said out loud. I can recite for you whole passages from the Bible. Psalm 63, "Oh God, thou art my God; early will I seek thee: my soul thirsteth for thee, my flesh longeth for thee in a dry and thirsty land, where no water is."

[*The phone rings.* EVA *goes to answer it.*]

"To see thy power and thy glory."

[*She picks up the phone.*]

Hello? Yeah, he's right here . . . Oh, hi, Mrs. Perch . . . I had to deliver towels. Clean sheets . . . She hung up.

PERCH: Susan?

EVA: Your wife.

PERCH: What did she say?

EVA: "Is this Dr. Perch's room . . . Is that you, Eva? Why are *you* in my husband's room?"

PERCH: Oh God, God, God. Things have gotten—they are going down the hill. She's divorcing me. Susan. She is.

[*He inhales nitrous oxide.*]

I can see why. I tried to adjust to the professional life. Be a good husband and father. I seem like a friendly man. But I stopped going along with the program. Phil Boone—but before that—other things—chloroform—before that . . . Phil Boone had a smell like dead skin and garbage. Came in with an impacted third molar. He was hurting, throbbing. Whole side of his mouth swollen with fever, infection. Didn't like showing his weakness. Started in claiming to be in on bombing the Negro church in Meridian. Bragged he lit the match. I thought I'd give him some ether to help with the pain of extraction. He kept removing the mask, kept talking, telling me it was time to dynamite the synagogue, go blow up the rabbi's house. I prepared a shot of sodium pentothal because he needed to go under the wire. I take in some of the nitrous oxide to lighten my mood.

[*He snorts cocaine.*]

And I pulled out all of his teeth! The molars, the fangs, central and lateral incisors. I'm used to blood on my hands, on my smock. A lot of blood comes from the mouth. It's full of veins. My secretary, Miss Burwell, helped me clean up. I explained it was an emergency. The teeth were life threatening and had to be extracted or Mr. Boone's chances of survival were some percent that wasn't much. I couldn't stop laughing. She never came back, Miss Burwell.

Although she did call Mrs. Boone to come pick up her husband.

It took a while for the lawyers and dentist examiners to get their ducks in a row. Now things have gotten bad. I've been hoping for some deus ex machina. Allowing the winds of oblivion to prevail. Oblivion. Has a good smell. Smells like chloroform. Ever tried it? Chloroform?

[PERCH *opens a bottle of chloroform and pours some on a towel.*]

EVA: What will it do to me?

PERCH: It can be lethal, cause brain impairment, insanity, visions, extreme dizziness. Chloroform comes with risks but it does stop sensibility.

EVA: Alright. Dr. Perch. My fiancé.

[*She breathes in the chloroform he holds over her mouth and nose.*]

It's sweet.

PERCH: Breathe in deep.

EVA: It's strong. It makes me feel . . .

[EVA *breathes in more and more chloroform. She staggers and dances around.*]

La-day, laa-daay . . . la, la, la, la . . . day.

[EVA *keels over.* PERCH *looks at her. He shakes her.*]

PERCH: Eva. You in there?

[EVA *shakes her head, confused.*]

Chloroform is something you should never probably do.

[PERCH *gets the ice bucket and dumps ice over* EVA.]

EVA: Shit! That's fucking cold!

[PERCH *takes the cloth of chloroform and inhales deep and hard.*]

PERCH: I got into the chloroform this past summer. Staying at the Jacksonian. Breathing in chloroform made me forget I should worry. I never ought to have let it happen. You know it's wrong but you want to do it more than you know it's wrong. And there is a second—[*static white noise*]—and the action has occurred and you did not choose to do or not do it. I feel at home in fog. Life makes sense.

[*White noise. Zigzag of lights. Time passes.*]

SCENE 11: THE MURDER

[*At the ice machine. Time: the night of the murder—December 17, 1964. Wearing a mink coat over her nightgown,* SUSAN *stands at the ice machine holding a crystal whiskey glass half-filled with scotch. She opens the lid, claws out pieces of ice, and drops them into her glass. The lid slams down.*]

[*In the bar/restaurant.* FRED *is cleaning up.* ROSY *enters wearing pajamas and wrapped in a blanket.*]

ROSY: Mama told me to wait in the car. She didn't want to leave me at home where someone might kill me.

[*In the motel room.* SUSAN *is banging on the door.* EVA *has passed out.* PERCH *is in a stupor.*]

SUSAN: Open the door, son of a bitch! Bill! Bill, let me in! It's Susan! Your wife! Bastard!

[PERCH *tries to dress himself and hide evidence of debauchery.*]

How dare you shut me out! I know you're in there! I hear you in there! Who else is there?! Some whore?! You have a whore!

[*She kicks and bangs on the door.*]

I'll kick down this door! Open the door! Fucking please! Let me in!

[PERCH *drags a practically unconscious* EVA *to the bathroom.* EVA *struggles a little and says something unintelligible but he dumps her inside and half shuts the door.*]

I'm your wife! I'm your wife! I'm your wife!

[PERCH *opens the door.* SUSAN *enters.*]

PERCH: Susan.

[SUSAN *looks at him. She sees all of the bizarre paraphernalia.*]

SUSAN: God. What? What is this?

PERCH: Things are easier without me.

[SUSAN *opens the bathroom door. She sees* EVA. *She steps into the bathroom.*]

SUSAN [*offstage*]: Is she dead?

PERCH: No.

SUSAN [*offstage*]: What's wrong with her?

PERCH: I believe she has been over-served.

SUSAN [*offstage*]: Ohmygod. God!

[SUSAN *sobs from the bathroom.* PERCH *listens to her.* PERCH *dresses himself with strange detachment. Sound of water rushing from the sink.*]

[*In the bar/restaurant.* ROSY *sits at a table. She is still.*]

FRED: I'm wondering, Rosy, if you are dehydrated?

ROSY: I'm thirsty.

FRED: I could see it.

[*He brings her a glass of water.*]

Here's some water.

[ROSY *doesn't drink.*]

Pinch your skin. If it stays up like a wall, it means you are dehydrated.

[ROSY *doesn't respond.* FRED *pinches her arm.*]

No. You're not dehydrated.

ROSY: Don't pinch my skin.

FRED: It was just a test to see if you were dehydrated.

[ROSY *pinches her skin. It does not stand up like a wall.*]

ROSY: I'm not dehydrated.

FRED: No.

[FRED *goes behind the bar and pours himself a drink.*]

ROSY: My parents . . .

FRED: What?

ROSY: My parents are divorcing.

FRED: Yeah.

ROSY: Fred?

FRED: Huh?

ROSY: I'll go away with you. Soon if you want.

FRED: Go where? I'm not going.

ROSY: You're going. To save your own skin. You should take me away and I would never return.

FRED: Your folks would be upset. They would miss you.

ROSY: Because I was gone, they would miss me in their minds. Because I was gone. Would you give me the ring?

FRED: What ring?

ROSY: The one you gave Eva.

FRED: I don't have it.

ROSY: I know you have it. I know where you got it from.

FRED: Where?

ROSY: From the Texaco lady. Off her ring finger. We'll use the money you stole that night. All the money, where you killed the cashier. Where you shot her in the throat.

FRED: What did Eva tell you?

ROSY: Nothing. I surmised it. I see through people. Involuntarily. Even when I shut my eyes.

FRED: Maybe we could go somewhere. To greener pastures.

ROSY: My parents are divorcing and then I'll be deserted. I won't be deserted. Take me away and I will not talk and tell anyone what you have done.

FRED: You really want to go with me?

ROSY: Yeah.

[FRED *watches her from behind the bar.*]

FRED: Come here, Rosy. I want you to come here behind the bar and let me show you something.

ROSY: What?

FRED: Don't ask what. Just come here.

[ROSY *stands.*]

> Leave the blanket. If you really want me to take you away, you
> have to trust me.

[ROSY *removes the blanket and walks up to the bar.*]

> I've got something for you. Right here. But you have to come back
> here to get it. Come on.

[ROSY *goes behind the bar.*]

ROSY: What?

FRED: I've got a ring for you.

[*He gives her the same ring he gave* EVA *earlier.*]

ROSY: That's nice. I've always wanted something around my finger.

FRED: Good.

[ROSY *puts the ring on her finger and pulls it off; puts it on, off, on.*]

ROSY: I like putting my finger in this little gold hole.

FRED: Rosy?

ROSY: Yeah?

FRED: Do you really want to be with me? Go away with me?

ROSY: And never return.

FRED: Prove to me you want to be with me. Show me. Feel this right here.

[FRED *exposes himself to* ROSY.]

ROSY: No.

FRED: Just touch it with your finger. Go on. Do it, Rosy. I want you to.

[*She lightly touches him.*]

ROSY: There.

FRED: Hold it. It's different than you think.

ROSY: We'll go away?

FRED: To greener pastures. A place you won't recognize. Now take all of it in your hand.

[ROSY *holds him for three beats then lets go.*]

ROSY: There, I did it.

FRED: How did it feel?

ROSY: Like an animal born too soon.

FRED: Rosy—

[ROSY *moves away from him. She comes from behind the bar and goes to get her blanket.*]

ROSY: Fred . . .

FRED: What?

ROSY: After you kill me, don't take back the ring.

[*A moment between them.*]

FRED: I won't kill you. Of course I won't. You know that. I'm not like that. I'm good.

[*In the motel room. The sound of water running.* PERCH *files his nails. Offstage* SUSAN's *crying is subsiding. The sound of running water stops.* SUSAN *enters from the bathroom wiping tears off her face with the arm of her fur coat.*]

SUSAN: This is sick. All of it.

PERCH: I agree.

SUSAN: What is she doing here?

PERCH: The things people do.

SUSAN: Were you intimate with her?

PERCH: I looked into her mouth.

SUSAN: You're trash. Why did I marry into trash? Motherfucking trash!

[SUSAN *goes to attack him.* PERCH *hits* SUSAN, *almost for the sport of it.* SUSAN *gasps with pain.*]

All you do—you hurt people! You are a people hurter! That's why they took your dental license away. To stop you from hurting people.

PERCH: I'm a good dentist. That's the one thing I can swear is true. I'm a good dentist.

SUSAN: You're not *allowed* to be a dentist. Everyone knows. They've dismantled you and you're not a dentist. You're not allowed to dispense toothpaste, hand out toothpicks in a box! You have failed in every way a man can fail!

[SUSAN *grabs the Christmas tree and slings it in his direction.*]

I'm divorcing you. I'm divorcing you because you have nothing to provide! You provide nothing.

PERCH [*overlapping*]: Parasite! Leech. Sucking my blood. Living off me, all this time.

SUSAN: There's no blood to suck! Grown man can't support his family. Your KKK daddy's sending you checks.

PERCH: That's lies.

SUSAN: You're lies. Full of hate like him.

[SUSAN *grabs a sheet.*]

Here's your sheet! Join the lynching! Be like your daddy! Join the KKK!

[SUSAN *slings the bedsheet over his head. Throughout the following,* PERCH *removes the sheet and douses it with chloroform.*]

Kill, bomb, tie an engine block to the body and throw it in the swamp! Let the terror—the terror—

[PERCH *grabs* SUSAN. *She struggles to get away.* PERCH *shakes her violently.*]

—purify our blood . . . Rosy . . . Rosy . . .

[PERCH *covers her face with the sheet soaked in chloroform and strangles her. He bangs her head against the wall three times—the last time very hard.* SUSAN *stops struggling and goes limp.* PERCH *removes the sheet.* SUSAN's *head is bleeding. He holds her in his arms a moment.*]

PERCH: You're fine. Just fine. Wake up. Susan. Baby. Pretty girl. Tell me something.

[PERCH *sits her up.*]

SUSAN: Hot. Thirsty. Hot.

PERCH: Let's get you out of this coat. It's too hot. There.

[PERCH *partly removes her coat.*]

Yes. Better?

SUSAN: Thirsty. Water.

[PERCH *reaches for the empty ice bucket. He gets up and exits to the ice machine.*]

Water. Please. Water.

[*Lights up on the ice machine. Time: a return to the beginning scene of the play.* PERCH *stands by the ice machine. He has blood on his hands and shirt. He violently digs the ice bucket ito the ice. There is the sound of ice crashing. He holds the ice in the bucket and stares out for no more than a moment.* PERCH *exits.*]

[*Lights up on the motel room.* SUSAN *is still. She feels the blood on her head. She says something we cannot understand.* ROSY *enters the room wearing the blanket.*]

ROSY: Mama? What happened?

SUSAN: Thirsty.

Thirsty . . . Water.

ROSY: Daddy.

[ROSY *exits.*]

SUSAN: Water . . .

[SUSAN*'s movements are discombobulated, like an insect that has almost been killed but not quite. She says something we cannot understand.*]

SCENE 12: AFTER AND BEFORE THE MURDER

[*Sound of sirens. Red lights flood across the sky. Chaotic noise of police cars, ambulances arriving.* ROSY *enters wearing the blanket.*]

ROSY: The time is . . . It's not Christmas. It's near around before— before Christmas. A murder happened. At the motel. The Jacksonian Motel.

Daddy called the authorities to come.

I gave the police the filling-station lady's ring. But it was too late.

Fred ran off. He disappeared.

Eva lost her mind to the chloroform.

Mama died alone in the room.

Daddy is in jail waiting on the gas chamber.

For a long time I knew my father was in trouble and my mother was not well, still I wanted to be together in the family.

If tonight did not happen I expect we could work things out. We'd make an effort. A sincere effort. And things would be changed. There still would be time.

[*Lights up on the ice machine. Time: June 1964, daytime.* PERCH *enters with a 7 Up and a Coke. He opens the drinks at the ice machine.*]

PERCH: Rosy, I've got your 7 Up! You need a drink on this hot day. Cool you off, Little Buddy.

[ROSY *enters wearing shorts. She seems younger and lighter than we have seen her throughout the play.*]

ROSY: Yes, sir, thank you.

[PERCH *hands* ROSY *the bottle of soda.*]

PERCH: It's going to be the Fourth of July soon enough. It will be nice to see some fireworks.

ROSY: Will you come home for the Fourth of July?

PERCH: Do you want me home?

ROSY: Yes.

PERCH: Good.

ROSY: Back when I was real little you—

PERCH: What?

ROSY: Do you remember at the zoo?

PERCH: The Jackson zoo?

ROSY: I was looking down at the rhinoceroses and my hat fell off my head. You jumped over the wall to get it.

PERCH: I don't believe I would jump in a wild animal pit.

ROSY: You did. Mama screamed. I thought a rhinoceros would gut you. But you climbed up the wall of dirt and hauled yourself out of the pit. People were cheering you because you had risked your life to save my hat.

PERCH: Well, it's possible. It's entirely possible.

ROSY: I remember—back when I was little.

PERCH: . . .

ROSY: Are you coming home?

PERCH: Yes.

ROSY: When?

PERCH: Maybe today.

ROSY: Good.

PERCH: Maybe today.

ROSY: Today.